IMAGES
of Rail

MACON TERMINAL STATION:
ITS PREDECESSORS
AND ITS RAILROADS

This 1912 photograph shows downtown Macon, looking down Cherry and Third Streets. This small Southern town of less than 50,000 was home to Macon Terminal Station, which any town many times the size of Macon would have been proud to have. (Courtesy Middle Georgia Regional Library.)

ON THE COVER: It was 1947. World War II was over. America's love affair with its private automobile had taken a chunk out of passenger train ridership. Airlines were stretching their wings, and motor coaches were rolling down the highways, all wreaking havoc on the plagued railroads. In an attempt to restore its business, the Central of Georgia Railway reequipped its *Nancy Hanks II* and *Man o' War* streamliners with new diesel locomotives and cars. To ensure success, the railroad simultaneously cut its fares drastically. Prior to the *Nancy Hanks II's* first day of operation on July 17, 1947, the railroad sent the trains on an eight-day tour across the state of Georgia. The *Nancy* is seen here on July 9 just outside Macon Terminal Station as it makes its debut. Across the state, 45,000 people walked through the trains, and they initially were a great success. Sadly, it was a success that would not endure. (Courtesy Central of Georgia Railway Historical Society, American Car & Foundry Company photograph.)

IMAGES
of Rail

MACON TERMINAL STATION: ITS PREDECESSORS AND ITS RAILROADS

David H. Steinberg on behalf of the
Middle Georgia Regional Library

ARCADIA
PUBLISHING

Published by Arcadia Publishing
Charleston, South Carolina

Printed in the United States of America

Library of Congress Control Number: 2018965628

For all general information, please contact Arcadia Publishing:
Telephone 843-853-2070
Fax 843-853-0044
E-mail sales@arcadiapublishing.com
For customer service and orders:
Toll-Free 1-888-313-2665

Visit us on the Internet at www.arcadiapublishing.com

To Allen Tuten and Arnold Eaves, Central of Georgia Railway Historical Society; and Muriel M. Jackson, Alicia Owens, and staff, Middle Georgia Regional Library—You made it possible!

Contents

Acknowledgments

It is difficult to believe that this book has reached fruition in light of the immense difficulties that initially stood in its path. After Macon Terminal Station's history had been researched and I contemplated approaching Arcadia Publishing, I realized I did not have the necessary images to complement the text. Suffice it to say that several organizations and individuals were approached that did not share the author's interest and enthusiasm. This all changed dramatically when the Middle Georgia Regional Library and the Central of Georgia Railway Historical Society were contacted. The library's staff, Muriel M. Jackson, Oliver Bushey, and Alicia Owens, who worked so diligently on preparing the many images, as well as the Central of Georgia Historical Society's Allen Tuten and Arnold Eaves, paved the way for this book's success. It is to them that I extend my greatest gratitude and appreciation for allowing my dream to come true. There were others who directly contributed to the project. These include my good friend Warren Stephens, who drove down to Macon to take some needed photographs; Ed Mims, who not only provided some rare photographs that add much color to the book, but also encouragement; Toni Elliott, formerly with the Macon Transit Authority; Jay Batcha; Prof. Robert M. Craig, who shared his beautiful contemporary images of Terminal Station; Peter Wrocenski; Steve Storey; Lloyd Neal; Marvin Clemons; Jim Goolsby; and Richard Stewart. There were others who sincerely tried to help and greatly encouraged the author. These include Catherine Boland Erkkila, W.R. Jones, Jena Lapachinski, Bibb County tax commissioner S. Wade McCord, and fellow Arcadia authors Glenda Barnes Bozeman and James Barfield. Certainly not to be forgotten are Arcadia's Jeff Reutsche and Angel Hisnanick, who must be thanked for their patience with the author and their guidance, which steered this book to completion. To all of you and to anyone I may have inadvertently failed to mention—Thank you!

Unless otherwise noted, all images appear courtesy of the Middle Georgia Regional Library. Images that are courtesy of the Central of Georgia Railway Historical Society through Allen Tuten, its president, are indicated as (CGRHS).

INTRODUCTION

There is a common phrase that says first impressions count. After December 1, 1916, with the opening of Macon Terminal Station, at around 5:00 on any given afternoon, passengers arriving on one of the ten stub tracks or eight through-platform tracks in the large station could have easily surmised that the city was of some size and stature. As many as 10 passenger trains would have been lined up, either arriving or awaiting their departure to various destinations. Upon entering the station head house itself and seeing the beautiful edifice glistening in magnificent shades of marble, that first impression of a huge metropolis would have been reinforced. In reality, 1916 Macon was a small town of less than 50,000 inhabitants. It owed its existence and importance to the Ocmulgee River, which in the city's formative years had been used to ship out the mainstay commodity of cotton to worldwide markets. With the coming of the railroad, increased opportunities became available, and an even greater economic prosperity was realized in the region.

Macon's association with railroads began on December 23, 1833, with the chartering of the Monroe Railroad & Banking Company. By 1854, four individual railroads were operating out of Macon to Atlanta, Savannah, Americus, Albany, Columbus, and Milledgeville, each with a separate passenger facility. With pressure from the City of Macon and various civic organizations, on December 10, 1855, Macon's first general passenger depot, Union Depot, was in operation on Broadway (Fourth Street today) and Plum Street, which consolidated all passenger trains under one roof. As early as 1866, it was rumored that the Central of Georgia Railway was preparing to erect a new station on land formerly used by the old courthouse at the foot of Mulberry Street to replace the already ramshackle Union Depot. Nothing, however, progressed past the planning stage, and 36 more years were allowed to pass. On February 26, 1902, the *Macon Telegraph* announced that a new movement was underway to unify all passenger train operations. The proposal envisioned the enlarging of the existing Union Depot by adding three additional tracks and otherwise updating the structure. Two separate committees were formed, one from the city council and the other from the chamber of commerce, but nothing materialized. After an additional five years, in 1907, the two committees reconvened to examine the problem to no avail. On October 2, 1910, for a third time, a committee was formed to approach the railroads about the thorny issue. The April 13, 1911, *Macon Telegraph* reported that Macon was again pulling for a new station. By this late date, Union Depot was truly in need of replacement.

On June 13, 1912, a Central of Georgia official announced correctly that a new station was imminent, and boastfully remarked that, instead of the originally estimated $1 million cost, the railroads were prepared to expend two or three times more to properly complete the project. On December 12, it was incorrectly reported that the Central of Georgia Railway had purchased two acres in the vicinity of the existing depot on Broadway for the new facility.

In 1913, a chamber of commerce committee headed by A.J. Long prepared data substantiating the need to replace the long outdated 1855 edifice. It gained the attention of the Georgia Railroad Commission, predecessor to today's Georgia Public Service Commission, which ordered work to commence. With 76 daily trains making regular stops in a city of only 48,225 people, the request this time would not be ignored. A new Macon Terminal Station would become reality!

On July 9, 1914, the Macon Terminal Company was chartered for a period of 101 years for the purpose of financing and constructing a union passenger station with an authorized capital stock of $100,000. This stock was issued on July 29, 1915, at $33,300 each to the three proprietary companies that would jointly own the property: the Central of Georgia; the Georgia Southern & Florida (GS&F); and the Southern Railway, with bonds to be sold up to $3 million. The Georgia Railroad; the Macon & Birmingham; and the Macon, Dublin & Savannah (MD&S) were invited to use the new facility as tenants but not as proprietary lines. In the meantime, a mortgage was created on July 1, 1915, and the company acquired the 13-acre station site from the Central of Georgia Railway for $450,000. On that date, a 50-year operating agreement was entered between the Macon Terminal Company and the three joint proprietary companies and the trustee of the first mortgage, providing for the joint use of the station with operating expenses and other costs to be divided on a user basis.

The Georgia Railroad Commission and city authorities tacked on strict regulations that had to be met before construction could commence. The Macon City Charter also had to be amended to authorize the closing of Cherry Street, which would be the center point for the two-block-long terminal that would stretch from Plum Street to Mulberry Street. Rep. Wallace Miller introduced the necessary amendment in the 1914 legislature. Plans submitted by famous New York architect Alfred Fellheimer were accepted for the station's design. Overseeing actual construction was Fellheimer's personally chosen supervising architect, George Kruge. J. Henry Miller of Baltimore was selected as the station's contractor, while the entire terminal project was placed under the direction of C.K. Lawrence, chairman of the board of engineers of Macon Terminal Company, with engineer F.L. Hewitt in charge of construction. In early fall of 1915, actual work was poised to begin, but stalled when several weeks of agonizing litigation commenced. Property owners in the Cherry Street vicinity contended, and later substantiated in court, that their properties' values had been diminished with the closing of the thoroughfare. In a second litigation, property owners below Fifth and Pine Streets maintained that the proposed Pine Street overpass did not meet city charter prerequisites. This group, however, was not successful in proving their claim, and it was dismissed. With these obstacles finally laid aside, construction was underway in October 1915. As a *Macon Telegraph* reporter aptly put it, "the opening of the new Terminal Station will mean more to Macon probably than any other event of the last several years. It has come after several years of talk, more of dreaming, two of litigation and legislation."

Macon Terminal Station's architect, Alfred Fellheimer, had an affinity for Roman Empire architecture, which he prominently displayed throughout the station. The central arched windows, which allowed for an abundance of natural light, emulated the thermal windows used in Roman baths, and building material such as Tennessee marble was used in the main lobby and waiting room areas. Even ornate metal railings and carved limestone eagles, symbolic of the Roman Empire, were incorporated into the structure. These eagles were the craftsmanship of a German immigrant, Adolf Alexander Weinman, who became a renowned New York sculptor just after the turn of the 20th century. The corridor between the waiting room areas was created with elaborate vaults forming the ceiling, complemented with gilt molding. In keeping with Roman tradition, massive Ionic columns supporting carved eagles were positioned at the station's main entrance. Fellheimer saw to it that the building's stairways and balconies—even the most remote crevices of the structure—were equipped not with standard cast iron but with what one reporter described as a "lyrical composition of the iron monger's art."

Despite the superlatives that were used to describe the station's interior, a Macon journalist reported that in his opinion, the exterior appearance from an architectural standpoint was equal to that of any city in the South, but that the building was "but a simple dignified classic design clad in Bedford limestone with a red cement tile roof." In reality, however, the station's exterior had been fashioned after the beautiful Washington Union Station, while the interior resembled what Fellheimer had built for Utica, New York's, equally exquisite Union Station.

Entering the main building through the high-arched ticket lobby area, passengers who already had ticket in hand and no need to check baggage could go directly to their train via a tunnel beneath the platform tracks. In that lobby were general ticket offices with one specifically for Pullman ticket purchasers, as well as a barbershop, telephone and telegraph offices, a newsstand, and a drugstore. To the right of the lobby was the spacious seating area, specifically designed to be out of the way yet easily visible to people passing by. This waiting room and lobby, similar to most of the building's interior, was described in a souvenir brochure issued by the railroads as "warm, soft shade pink Tennessee marble with floors of southern marble and a ceiling of ornamental plaster." The wooden bench seating area in the waiting room was located in alcoves on either side of the main aisle between the ticket lobby and Passageway No. 2, leading to the street. Leading from the main waiting room, as was the custom in those days, was a separate waiting area for women. To allow for maximum ventilation during hot Georgia summers, the windows could be opened by means of racks and pinions and made to disappear into recesses in the walls, allowing for the passage of air through the full window area. A mezzanine floor was provided at track level above the kitchen and black lunchroom. This floor was solely for the use of railroad employees, with its own telegraph and register offices, lockers, report rooms, and restroom facilities. Also leading from the lobby were the stairs and elevator to reach the multitude of offices on the second and third floors for the Central of Georgia, Southern, GS&F, and Georgia railroad companies. As was also the custom in those days, a separate waiting room, dining room, and restrooms for black patrons were located left of the main terminal building. To save kitchen and pantry space, as well as the expense of hiring separate employees in each facility, both the white and black restaurants, operated by the Parker Railway News Company, shared a common kitchen.

At the rear was the 33-foot-wide concourse, stretching the entire 243-foot length of the building. An incline on the west side of the concourse ended at five local stub-end tracks and the baggage building. A similar incline on the east side of the concourse led to an additional five local stub-end tracks and the Railway Express Agency and US mail building. The baggage room was 112 feet long by 57 feet wide. A 23-foot-long section was dedicated strictly for the use of the US Postal Service. The express building east of the main terminal was 134 feet long by 57 feet wide. Terminal Station's heating and lighting plant was located in the baggage building.

The subway passage beneath the tracks to reach the platforms was especially well lighted and ventilated by a series of circular openings through which natural light and air were allowed to circulate. Like the rest of the building, the 36-foot-wide subway was also walled in Tennessee marble with a cement floor with benches along its length for the convenience of waiting passengers. There were eight through-passenger tracks above the subway, sheltered by steel butterfly-type overhead sheds. To reach train side required the use of steps, one of only two places in the entire station where passengers were required to use steps to go from one level to another. When the station opened, the platforms were built of wood instead of the normal concrete. This was necessary because of an eight-foot fill that was required to reach the elevation level needed at that point. After the earth settled, the permanent concrete platforms were positioned. Macon Terminal comprised a total 78,500 square feet, with a 55,000-square-foot roof area plus an additional 30,000 square feet of covered and platform areas.

Although the centerpiece of the 1916 construction was the new $600,000 Terminal Station building itself, a much larger amount of money was spent creating its approaches. Close to $2 million was expended to construct the necessary rail approaches for the Central of Georgia and Southern Railways. The Central of Georgia approach accounted for the bulk of the expense, requiring the construction of a 2,700-foot-long fill and a steel viaduct 1,540 feet in length as part of the new "Atlanta cut-off." This was necessary to allow trains to operate through the new station without the need for time-consuming backing in and out that had been required in the old Union Depot. The fill was constructed 2,700 feet from the new station to Bay Street, built on a 1.25 percent ascending grade, to allow a 22-foot vertical clearance where the new line crossed the lead to the freight warehouse on Bay Street. From Bay Street, the line was built with a viaduct section extending some 300 feet, which was constructed on a 0.41 percent ascending grade to reach the junction with the original main line. Of the total length of the 1,540-foot viaduct, 1,308 feet were built on an over eight-degree curve. Leaving Bay Street, the viaduct was built with two deck spans and a through span over the freight house lead. From the crossing of the freight house track, 30-foot deck girder spans were utilized to the crossing of the GS&F, where because of the flat angle intersection it was necessary to place the columns in bents parallel with the lower tracks. Beyond this, the line crossed two street intersections where a minimum of 12 feet 6 inches had to be maintained. At the intersection with Broadway, a through-grade span was used, and from Broadway to its end where the viaduct followed the line of Ash Street, it was necessary to support the heavy girder on columns set just back of the curb line. All the steel was fabricated and erected by the Virginia Bridge & Iron Company. The masonry was all plain concrete, except for the east abutment, which was reinforced trestle. The Southern Railway approach used a less extensive alignment consisting of an 800-foot fill between gravity retaining walls and ending with a reinforced concrete viaduct. The Atlanta cut-off was designed by Central of Georgia engineer J.B. Murdock and erected under the supervision of C.K. Lawrence, chief engineer for the Central of Georgia. Southern Railway's concrete viaduct was designed under the supervision of W.H. Wells, chief engineer of construction for the Southern.

With the newly created approaches to Macon Terminal Station, Central of Georgia trains from the east left the original line 3,000 feet east of the old Union Station and swung south to Terminal Station over a new double-track right-of-way; the old passenger track was now utilized strictly for freight trains. Trains from Savannah destined for Atlanta left the Macon Terminal tracks 1,200 west of the new station and, as above, traveled 2,700 feet to Bay Street where they passed over a 1,540-foot steel viaduct to connect with the original mainline tracks to Atlanta. Central of Georgia trains of the Columbus and Southwestern Divisions used Macon Terminal trackage for 800 feet, where they connected with the new double-track line that was built to Macon Junction to reach the original tracks. The GS&F and the Macon & Birmingham trains, both controlled by the same management, left Terminal Station over the same route as those of the Central of Georgia to Macon Junction, where they connected to their own home rails. Georgia Railroad Company trains used Central of Georgia tracks to a junction with its own rails at Mogul. Southern Railway now utilized the original tracks to its old Ocmulgee Street Station for freight, and its approach to the new Terminal Station left the existing line at a point about a half mile east of the old station via a fill some 800 feet long that passed over the freight house drive, the intersection of Ocmulgee and Fifth Streets, the drive to the new station, and the tracks heading to the MD&S freight house. Trains from Atlanta entered Terminal Station over this filled approach and viaduct over the tracks of the Central of Georgia to Macon Junction. From Macon Junction for approximately 1.5 miles, they used GS&F rails to a new connection to the main line.

After just one year of construction, the new station was ready for business in October 1916. However, it could not be opened due to more litigation brought by property owners living below Fifth and Pine Streets, who alleged that the Pine Street underpass did not meet city requirements. The property owners lost, but the four corporations that they represented were awarded $42,500 in damages.

On a sunny and fair Friday, December 1, 1916, at exactly 9:00 in the morning, the many years of waiting were ended when Macon Terminal Station was officially opened for business. Operating on a precise schedule, at exactly 9:35 a.m., Central of Georgia Train No. 8 from Albany, Georgia, took the honors to become the first train to enter the new facility. Because rails had not yet been readied above Pine Street, it was necessary for this initial train to operate past the station and back in as had been the custom until then. This train, however, made additional history, for it became the last one to have to perform this movement. At the throttle of Train No. 8 was engineer E.A. Scoville, with A. Johnson serving as conductor. The terminal's stationmaster, W.F. Whipple, was on the platform to meet the train, as was A.G. Reddy, one of Terminal Station's train callers. Also reported on duty were W.L. Chandler and John Stark, chief dispatcher and dispatcher, respectively. Of additional interest is the fact that with one exception, the Southern Railway's 12 daily trains had to continue to use the old Ocmulgee Street facility until January 7, 1917, when track work was completed that allowed its trains to enter the new Terminal Station.

Although no special ceremonies were held to commemorate the station's opening, many government and railroad officials were on hand for the celebration. These included members of the Georgia Railroad Commission who had come in from Atlanta. The *Macon Telegraph* noted that thousands of Maconites were on hand to witness the historic occasion. By the end of the day, some 74 trains had arrived and departed from Macon Terminal Station, vividly illustrating the reason the facility had become necessary.

With the advent of the private family vehicle and its offspring the motor coach, the beginning of the end for passenger train service began in the 1920s. World War II provided a temporary upsurge in rail business, but with the silencing of the guns and the improvements by then of the airplane, the end of widespread passenger train service was imminent. On April 30, 1971, Central of Georgia's *Nancy Hanks II* became the final passenger train to pull out of Macon Terminal Station.

After only 55 years, Macon Terminal Station's reason for being had come to a screeching halt.

These two rare photographs were taken in Macon sometime between 1870 and 1880. Above is an overall view of the Central of Georgia Railway roundhouse. Already in that early era, Macon was fast becoming an important railroad center. At least 18 stalls are visible; quite impressive for the time. Below is a portion of the railroad's Macon yard not far from the roundhouse. Notice the "cowcatcher" on the front of the engine. Its purpose was to do just that: keep cattle and livestock from being killed in the event they had a misunderstanding with the locomotive. The hope was that the animal would be pushed aside, thereby possibly saving its life. It also worked for people who did not have enough sense to stay away from a speeding locomotive.

One

MACON TRANSFORMS INTO A RAILROAD HUB

Macon owes its existence to cotton and the Ocmulgee River. Leading into the Atlantic Ocean, the Ocmulgee provided the primary route for the lucrative commodity to reach worldwide manufacturing centers. Beginning December 10, 1838, the river was joined by the Macon & Western Railroad (M&W). Initially operating only 25 miles to Forsyth, the goal of reaching Atlanta was achieved on August 18, 1846, when the *Atlanta Luminary* reported that the first train conveying some 300 passengers was met by thousands for a gala celebration. On August 24, 1872, the M&W was consolidated with the Central Railroad & Banking Company, creating a coveted through line from Savannah to the Georgia capital. Initially, the M&W maintained its passenger station near the intersection of Pine and Spring Streets.

The second railroad to reach Macon was the Central Railroad & Banking Company, which reached McCall's Mill Station, two and a half miles from Macon, on August 1, 1843, and shortly after was completed to East Macon, where a permanent station was located. When a bridge was built across the Ocmulgee River, a station was constructed in downtown Macon at the foot of Mulberry Street. This railroad, controlled by a holding company, the Richmond Terminal Company, was a prosperous system. However, after 1888, it was in financial disarray. On November 1, 1895, the railroad was sold at foreclosure and reorganized as the Central of Georgia Railway.

The third railroad to reach Macon was the Southwestern Railroad, which was chartered in December 1845 to build to the lower Chattahoochee River. Construction begun in 1848, progressed slowly, and by 1851 had only been readied from Macon to the Flint River at Oglethorpe, Georgia. This company maintained its initial passenger station at Pine and Fifth Streets. With a $75,000 gift by Americus, Georgia, citizens, the railroad entered that town in 1854. In 1857, the Southwestern purchased the line then under construction by the Georgia & Florida Railroad from Americus to Albany and rushed it to completion. The Georgia & Florida was consolidated into the Southwestern Railroad in late 1859. At Fort Valley in 1853, a branch was built west to meet the 50-mile unfinished Muscogee Railroad begun in 1847 as a Columbus-to-Macon route. When the Muscogee failed in 1853, the Southwestern stepped in and completed a connection to the Muscogee's eastern end at Butler in June of that year. On June 24, 1869, the Southwestern Railroad was itself leased to the Central of Georgia Railway.

The next railroad to enter Macon was the 1859-chartered Macon & Augusta Railroad. In 1873, the line was completed to Warrenton, where it connected with the Warren branch of the Georgia Railroad & Banking Company, which joined Georgia Railroad's mainline at Camak. From there, trains could operate directly into Augusta. The Macon & Augusta was leased to the Georgia Railroad & Banking Company in 1867 and in 1880 was bought outright by the Georgia Railroad. This company's initial wooden combination freight and passenger depot was located at Poplar Street near Sixth Street. After being abandoned, it became an oil warehouse. In May

1907, in preparation for locating Central of Georgia's new railroad shops, the old landmark was reduced to a memory.

Macon's fifth railroad, the Macon & Brunswick Railroad, opened for business in 1867 when 50 miles of track were readied from Macon to Hawkinsville. The real purpose of this line was to reach the Atlantic Ocean at Brunswick, Georgia. With the help of New York investors and a state-endorsed $2.5 million bond sale, the 174-mile road was rushed to completion on January 1, 1870. On September 18, 1881, the Macon & Brunswick was secured by the East Tennessee, Virginia & Georgia Railroad (ETV&G), which, in 1895, became an important part of the Southern Railway Company.

This sixth railroad, the ETV&G, had been chartered in 1869 as a consolidation of the East Tennessee & Georgia, operating between Knoxville and Dalton, Georgia, and the East Tennessee & Virginia Railroad, operating between Knoxville, Tennessee, and Bristol, Tennessee-Virginia. In 1881, the ETV&G purchased the Georgia Southern Railroad, operating between Dalton and Selma, Alabama, and in the same year bought the 174-mile Macon & Brunswick. To connect these lines, the ETV&G built its Atlanta Division, 158 miles from Rome to Macon, completing the segment in 1882. The first train operated on October 8 of that year from Chattanooga via Dalton and Rome to reach Atlanta and Macon.

The Covington & Macon Railroad became the seventh to enter Macon. This line was chartered to connect Macon with Covington on the existing Georgia Railroad. Construction began in 1886, and by June 1887 had reached Monticello. It was then decided to alter the terminus to Athens, Georgia, a move designed to attract new investment in the faltering enterprise. By March 1888, the railroad was completed to Madison. The final 105 miles were built by the end of the year and the company was opened on January 15, 1889. Traffic failed to materialize, and the line was sold at auction on May 21, 1891. Two days later, the railroad was reorganized as the Macon & Northern Railroad Company. In 1894, it was leased to the Richmond & Danville and Georgia Central Railroad & Banking Company. On October 31, 1895, the Central bought out the line entirely.

Macon's railroad growth was far from over. The eighth railroad to enter the Macon market was the Georgia Southern & Florida Railroad. It was chartered in 1885 to build an over 285-mile line from Macon to Palatka, Florida. It made its debut in February 1889 when the line was completed as far as Valdosta and was opened the full distance to Palatka by March of the following year. Beginning in 1891, the company encountered financial difficulties and went into receivership until 1895, when the line was reorganized as the Georgia Southern & Florida Railway. At that time, it came under the control of the new Southern Railway Company. In 1902, the GS&F bought the Atlantic, Valdosta & Western Railway, operating between Valdosta and Jacksonville. It also owned the Hawkinsville & Florida Southern Railway and the Macon & Birmingham Railroad, which became the ninth line to enter Macon and was completed in January 1891 to connect Macon with LaGrange, Georgia. Initially, it maintained its own passenger station at Fifth and Pine Streets in downtown Macon, but as of January 14, 1912, the Macon & Birmingham switched over to Union Depot. The line was abandoned in 1922–1923.

The final railroad to tap the Macon market was the Macon & Dublin Railroad. Chartered in 1885 to connect the two namesake towns, it opened up an area known for its famous Georgia peaches. In 1890, the name was changed to the more prestigious Macon, Dublin & Savannah Railroad. By the end of 1891, the line was opened to Dublin. Work was not resumed on the remaining portion until 10 years later, in April 1901. In March 1902, the line reached Vidalia, Georgia, its ultimate terminus. Although Savannah was never reached, because the Seaboard Airline Railway had an existing 92-mile route from Vidalia to Savannah, Macon secured its second through route to the important Savannah destination.

These 10 trunk railroads made Macon into an important rail hub.

There are no known photographs of the first Central of Georgia Railway station, built in East Macon in 1843. This drawing, surely out of size and proportion, gives an idea of what it purportedly looked like. Additionally, no photographs have been found of the small passenger depots mentioned in chapter one's introduction.

This extremely rare image, taken between 1870 and 1880, is believed to show the interior of Macon's Central of Georgia Railway roundhouse.

Although the railroads became the primary mover of people across the country, they were initially built for commerce: the hauling of farm products and the movement of industrial commodities. In this 1900s image, Macon's impressive Macon, Dublin & Savannah freight depot, then located on Riverside Drive, is pictured. In later years, it was used by the *Macon Telegraph & News* as its warehouse.

It is May 31, 1886, the day before the Central Railroad & Banking Company's track gauge was changed from 5 feet to the standard 4 feet, 8.5 inches. This probably explains why so many locomotives are lined up at the shops. The large tower is believed to be a water tank.

Little information about this photograph, like so many other images from the 1880s, has survived. The men are unidentified, and the reason behind their gathering is left to the imagination. What is known is that this is a Central of Georgia train, somewhere near Macon.

This 1901 photograph was taken in Gallemore in Twiggs County, between Macon and Danville, Georgia. Note the men with rifles and the dogs. It seems they are going to a hunt; the women will perhaps do some picnicking. An MD&S train has brought the group to its destination.

The *Nancy Hanks* was the name of a famous Central of Georgia train in later years. Initially, however, the name was given to Central of Georgia's new American-type Locomotive No. 1592, which the railroad had just placed into service. This image dates to the 1890s.

A doubleheader GS&F special has just brought a group of picnickers from Macon to Bonaire, Georgia, 23 miles south. Several hundred people, it seems, will have a fine outing this day!

The exact location of this rare image is not known; however, a Macon & Western Railroad passenger train, operating between Macon and Atlanta, is pictured. The photograph was taken no later than 1872, which was when the M&W was consolidated into the Central of Georgia Railway & Banking Company.

This is yet another image of a passenger train operating either toward or away from Macon. The location and date are unknown, but the No. 1610 is heading a Central of Georgia speeding train.

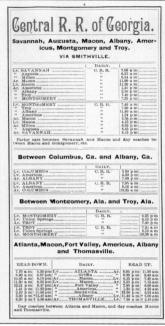

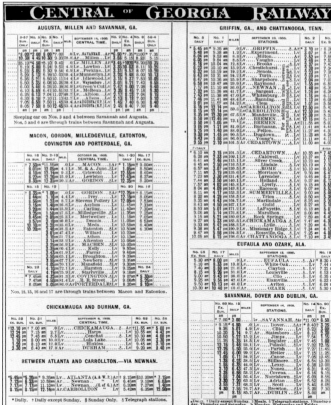

These early timetables are dated February 10, 1893, and already list the *Nancy Hanks*, which would become one of the South's most beloved passenger trains. Macon was on its way to becoming a major railroad hub. (Both, courtesy CGRHS.)

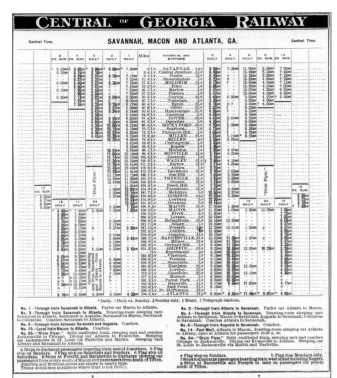

These schedules date from October 1908. Macon was now being served by several named trains and was fast becoming an important rail hub.

The original caption for this image notes that these are GS&F engineers in Macon Central Park around 1910. The occasion for the gathering is unknown.

The American-type steam locomotive with its 4-4-0 wheel arrangement proved to be far superior to what had been created until then. By the late 1870s, three quarters of all steam locomotives were powered by this engine. Even the small MD&S utilized this type of motive power, as seen here in Macon shortly after the turn of the 20th century. (Courtesy Steve Storey and Lloyd Neal.)

Two

MACON'S FIRST
UNION STATION

By 1854, four railroads were operating in Macon. The Macon & Western to Atlanta was operating out of its Pine and Spring Streets station; the Central of Georgia Railway into Savannah maintained its station at the foot of Mulberry Street; the Southwestern Railroad, operating then to Americus, Georgia, had its depot at Fifth and Pine Streets; and the Macon & Augusta, operating the 22 miles into Milledgeville, had its station at Poplar and Sixth Streets. With each line maintaining its own depot and separate facilities, a considerably undesirable situation, the City of Macon and various civic organizations began to clamor for the creation of a central union station in the city. To give the project more impetus, the City of Macon offered to contribute a large amount of money to the project. The way had already been cleared legally for the creation of a joint Macon passenger terminal when, on February 11, 1850, the Georgia General Assembly approved legislation that allowed for the creation of such a station, contingent upon the city's approval. This approval came on January 24, 1851, through legislation passed by the city and accepted by Mayor J.H.R. Washington. For the privilege of operating into a joint passenger depot, each railroad agreed to an annual payment of $5,000. In 1854, the new general passenger depot, Union Depot, was under construction at the corner of Broadway (Fourth Street today) and Plum Street downtown. The station's design closely resembled Atlanta's passenger depot that had been built in 1853, and the West Point, Georgia, depot of the Atlanta & West Point Railroad that had been built a year later. Constructed by the Central of Georgia, the station was built on property that measured 400 by 100 feet, and the station itself occupied 325 by 87 feet. Moore, Logan & Mears constructed it; James A. Knight, who had also designed Atlanta's Union Depot, was its architect, and James B. Ayres, described as a master builder in brick and stone, took care of the masonry. The two-story, 45-by-100-foot station house was constructed of brick and was surrounded by a brick wall with a wrought iron gate, measuring 43 by 100 feet. The tin roofing was laid by William J. McElroy & Company. A dining room 97 by 28 feet was on the second floor. The 10 rooms on the first floor offered separate waiting rooms for male and female patrons, as was the custom, along with the necessary baggage rooms, ticket offices, washrooms, and porters' rooms. The shed area covered three stub-end tracks, while side tracks on either side of the station were used exclusively by the Central of Georgia trains. The Central owned the station, which cost the railroad close to $100,000 to construct. The first train to use the facility was a Southwestern Railroad train that arrived from Fort Valley at 11:00 a.m. on December 10, 1855, although the station was not officially opened until December 13. All trains had to back into the station.

On the afternoon of October 29, 1891, at 3:30 p.m., a disastrous fire broke out in the station. This caused an explosion near the ticket offices that quickly consumed the entire car shed, a couple of Southwestern Railroad coaches, and an inspection car. One person, Henry Sloan, perished in the inferno. Although the October 30, 1891, *Macon Telegraph* pleaded in its editorial that a new depot "that has long been agitated and contemplated" should now be decided upon, it was not to be. At that time, the Central of Georgia Railway, which owned the station, was controlled by the Richmond & Danville holding company, which secured the fire insurance money. It promised a new station would be constructed, but in the meantime, it did not do any building. It took until the spring of 1892 for the Central to secure the funds; it immediately commenced construction on April 19, 1892. At that time, a contract for Union Depot's rebuilding was awarded by depot superintendent Curran to R.C. Wilder & Sons and stipulated that construction had to begin within 10 days. Total cost of construction to rebuild the station was listed as $25,000, but the contract awarded to Wilder & Sons did not include the rebuilding of the large iron shed overhanging the platform tracks, which was negotiated with another company. By agreement, the shed area had to be ready by September 1 and Wilder & Sons had to have the station head house completed by July 1. Keeping close to that schedule, Union Depot reopened on July 7, 1892. The station had retained its original design except for the roof, which now was pitched instead of being rounded. The roof was composed of slate and glass, the latter forming a skylight 360 feet in length by 12 feet in width. The shed area was increased to 390 feet, and an additional fourth track was added to the station, which itself was modernized with the latest design in benches. A ladies' parlor room was added with luxurious carpets and other up-to-date furnishings. In the ladies' general waiting room, three windows were cut into the brick to allow them to see the trains arrivals and departures. A new brick baggage room 30 feet in length was built along the east side of the station as well as another 30-foot-long mailroom. On the west side, a car inspectors' and office supply room of brick was also built. New, heavier rails were laid in the station area under the shed.

As early as 1866, rumor had it that the Central of Georgia Railway was interested in replacing what was then already being called the antiquated Union Depot. Nothing, however, would take place until 1916, when the new Macon Terminal Station became reality. In the interim, in December 1910, the station was freshly painted and additional renovations were made. On September 5, 1911, improved lighting was installed: 10 tungsten 500-watt lamps replaced the old antiquated system, along with four 250-watt lamps that were positioned in pairs in front of the depot and the baggage room. Beginning Sunday, January 14, 1912, the station secured an additional tenant when the Macon & Birmingham Railroad closed its separate Fifth and Pine Street Station and began to use Union Depot. On that same date but one year later, in 1913, steam escaping from one of Union Depot's overhead pipes was mistaken for a fire and firemen were called to the scene to extinguish the blaze. "Let 'er burn" many cried out in the quickly assembled crowd that came to witness the supposed inferno. "We need a new station," they all screamed to the firemen, who sadly advised the crowd that there was actually no fire.

Union Depot was destined to serve Macon until Terminal Station opened on December 1, 1916. The building was then remodeled into a theatrical productions auditorium. Traveling artists were featured for seven years until 1925, when the historic relic was torn down and laid to eternal rest.

During its tenure, Union Depot saw the likes of Jefferson Davis, Stephen A. Douglas, and US presidents Woodrow Wilson, William McKinley, Theodore Roosevelt, and William Howard Taft.

The General Passenger Depot, located at Fourth and Plum Streets, is pictured in 1876. Opened on December 10, 1855, it sported a two-story head house and a three-track passenger shed with a side track on either side of the station, for five loading tracks. The waiting rooms were at street level, while a dining room occupied the second floor.

This view of the 1855 General Passenger Depot is from 1877. The stub-end depot made it mandatory for every train using the facility to back in and then head out, creating a rather time-consuming bottleneck with which the local railroad people were never content.

This is yet another view of Macon's 1855 Union Depot, seen here in 1877. By this date, Macon had a local street railway system (the Macon Street Railroad Company) and telephone service, as well as maybe electricity. It is not known whether the streetlamps operated on gas or electricity.

This postcard not only shows Union Depot but also what appears to be Macon's entire fire department apparatus fleet. On October 29, 1891, almost the entire fire department was needed when an inferno practically destroyed the entire shed section of the station.

The rear side of Union Depot is captured in this 1870s view. Compare this image with the photograph below and note the changes made to the station after the disastrous 1894 fire.

This c. 1912 photograph shows Union Depot's shed area with an idling steam train. Since only Central of Georgia trains utilized the two outside station tracks, it can be assumed that this is indeed a Central of Georgia train.

A 4-4-0 locomotive and most likely its engineer and conductor pose for a portrait. This Central of Georgia train is awaiting its highball signal to head out of Macon, possibly to Atlanta or Savannah.

This photograph shows two trains at Union Depot's shed area. The 4-6-0 10-wheeler looks impatient and ready to go with its full head of steam. Engineer J.D. Lamon poses in the cab of his MD&S locomotive.

A Central of Georgia Class E 4-4-0 is pictured at Macon Union Depot. The date is April 1916, and the train is destined for either Atlanta or Savannah. (Courtesy Steve Storey and Lloyd Neal.)

The immaculately clean Central of Georgia No. 1576 sits at Union Depot. It is obvious that the railroad company was proud of its passenger train operations in March 1916. (Courtesy Steve Storey and Lloyd Neal.)

In May 1916, a Georgia Railroad employee attends to the needs of his locomotive by oiling it before commencing his next run. No. 61 will soon be on its way to Union Depot to pull its train to Camak with a connection to Augusta. (Courtesy Steve Story and Lloyd Neal.)

A Central of Georgia Class P 4-6-2 No. 1657 looks ready and eager to commence its next journey. It is April 1, 1916, and the locomotive is just outside the original Union Depot, waiting to couple to its train. (Courtesy Steve Story and Lloyd Neal.)

GS&F 4-6-0 No. 163 sits in Macon Union Depot ready to head to Valdosta and Florida points. This is another image captured in March 1916, just months before GS&F trains switched over to the new Terminal Station. (Courtesy Steve Storey and Lloyd Neal.)

The nickname "Suwanee River Route" identifies this locomotive as a GS&F possession. The 4-4-0 locomotive was very popular in the 1880s and was used by virtually every major railroad at that time. (Courtesy Steve Storey and Lloyd Neal.)

"Maude," Central of Georgia's beloved saddle tank locomotive, is seen switching a locomotive on the turntable in Macon's yard. No. 8 began its life as No. 1108, a Baldwin-built 1889 product. In 1925, it was renumbered the No. 8. Today, it sits proudly in Savannah at the Roundhouse Railroad Museum.

Central of Georgia No. 509, built by Baldwin in 1906, has been in Macon's Central Park since 1959. A plaque at the site honors Benny A. Scott, a community leader and the railroad's first black fireman, who worked this locomotive's last run.

Three

ETV&G's Ocmulgee Street Station

In 1881, the East Tennessee, Virginia & Georgia Railroad entered Macon with its purchase of the existing Macon & Brunswick Railroad. The following year, on October 4, it completed its own Rome via Atlanta to Macon Division. Research indicates that ETV&G passenger trains initially used the existing Broadway (Fourth Street today) and Plum Street Union Passenger Depot, but that it planned in time to construct its own facility. This is substantiated in the 1882 *Railroad Gazette*, which noted in an interview with J.W. McCracken, who was in charge of building the ETV&G from Macon to Atlanta, that $216,000 had been paid out for properties on which to erect some 20 "tasty modern" wooden stations along the line. An additional $75,000 had been allocated to erect these stations' buildings. Mention was made that more money would be expended on the "city depots" that would be built, and although not mentioned by name, these surely referred to stations in the larger towns of Atlanta and Macon.

Various railroad periodicals from the era give the impression that it took an additional four years before the ETV&G could finalize its Macon station plans. This was surely because of overspeculation in railroad construction, which brought the railroad into receivership in 1895. The March 16, 1886, *Macon Weekly Telegraph*, however, was finally able to report that a passenger depot and warehouse were to be erected soon by the ETV&G. The March 30 edition reported in an interview with B.W. Wrenn, general passenger agent and ticket agent for the railroad, that the Macon depot plans were about completed and work would commence shortly. The September 21, 1886, edition noted that surveyors were at work locating the foundation and taking dimensions for the new ETV&G Macon station. Close examination of the top image on page 35 reveals a concrete tablet embedded in the chimney just above the first floor of the station inscribed "1886."

ETV&G's Macon station was constructed on Ocmulgee and Fifth Streets, today's Martin Luther King Jr. Boulevard and Riverside Drive, some three-fourths of a mile from the Union Passenger Depot. The station was a simple two-story frame building that sported a three-story tower and an overhanging roof below the second-story windows. The overhanging roof provided a measure of protection against the elements since the station had no covered platforms along its two tracks. When constructed, it amply provided the necessary passenger requirements for the era. Thomas Henley had been in charge of the Hawkinsville, Georgia, depot but was promoted to fill the Macon stationmaster position effective April 1, 1886.

With the takeover by the Southern Railway Company of the East Tennessee, Virginia & Georgia Railroad in 1895, the *Macon Telegraph* for October 23 of that year correctly reported that the Southern was busy laying track from the Ocmulgee Street Station to Union Passenger Depot. The paper, however, erroneously reported that Southern Railway trains would begin to enter the Union Passenger Depot facility with completion of the construction. The precise reason why this did not happen is uncertain but is believed to be because Southern Railway and the Central of Georgia, which owned Union Depot, could not come to terms on the rental fee for use of the facility. In 1898, rumor had it that Southern Railway was prepared to enter Union Passenger Depot, but nothing happened. On March 29, 1902, the *Macon Telegraph* reported for yet a third time that Southern Railway was seriously considering the building of a new station at the foot of Second Street. The $60,000 price tag tacked on the site, however, quickly sobered the railroad, and once again, no action was taken to implement a station site change. In the meantime, continuing to use the Ocmulgee Station as tenants were the Macon & Northern and Macon & Dublin Railroads. Southern Railway was destined to remain in the Ocmulgee Street Station until the doors to the new Macon Terminal Station opened on December 1, 1916, and all passenger lines began to use the united facility.

By the turn of the 20th century, the Ocmulgee Street Station had gained the infamous reputation, described by the local *Macon Telegraph*, as being nothing more than "a little dingy smoky structure" that needed to be immediately replaced. In the meantime, starting August 17, 1902, the Macon & Dublin Railroad, by then renamed the Macon, Dublin & Savannah Railroad, began a new through service between Macon and Savannah, per its name. MD&S trains began to operate over its own rails as far as Vidalia, Georgia, where they switched over to rails owned by the Seaboard Airline Railway to continue to Savannah.

Of note is the interesting "Shuttle Train" service that the MD&S provided soldiers, effective December 18, 1916, between Ocmulgee Station and nearby Camp Wheeler. Operating between Ocmulgee Station and Seven Mile Post at approximately every hour and twenty-five minute intervals, the service provided a convenient way for the up to 29,000 officers and enlisted men to enter and leave the city. How long the service ran is not known, but surely it did not last after the men left for France. The last train had to leave Macon for the return trip to the base no later than 9:15 p.m., and the final train back to Macon could not leave the base after 10:00 p.m. This was at the request of the base commander General Kernan, who insisted that his men be back in the barracks by 10:00 p.m. to get their needed sleep.

On December 1, 1916, Macon's colossal Terminal Station was opened to an elated city. Because some track work remained to be completed, with two exceptions, Southern Railway trains could not enter Terminal Station until over a month later on January 7, 1917. At that time, the building was abandoned for railroad use. The station was left to stand until March 1946, when Southern Railway announced plans for carrying out a four-point program for improvements in the Macon area. The railroad advised that the 60-year-old landmark would be torn down. Shortly after, the Macon Lumber & Wrecking Company began salvaging whatever useful materials could be had from the doomed structure. Only in history books and in the memories of those old enough to have witnessed the station would there be proof that Ocmulgee Street Station had ever existed on the site.

The East Tennessee, Virginia & Georgia Railroad opened Macon's Ocmulgee Street Station in 1886. In this 1894 scene, one of its passenger trains is depicted at the station. A horse-and-buggy hack is ready to transport any potential passengers.

It is after 1894. The original ETV&G Railroad has now become the Southern Railway. Its train is just pulling into the station, and passengers prepare to embark for Atlanta.

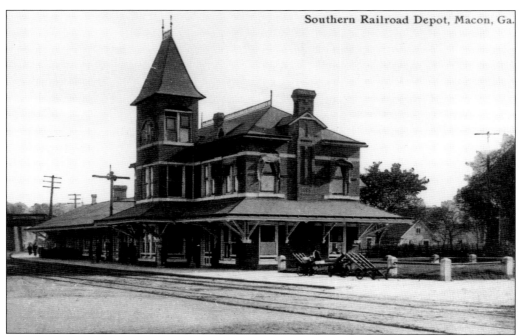

In later years, Ocmulgee Street Station gain the infamous title of "a little dingy smoky structure." This postcard, however, depicts a well-kept structure. The overhead bridge in the background carries Central of Georgia's mainline trains over the tracks below for safety purposes.

This 4-6-0 locomotive is typical of the motive power that operated in and out of Ocmulgee Street Station. Few other images exist of this obscure, but important, Macon railroad station.

Four

MACON TERMINAL STATION IN ITS FULL GLORY

The 1800s had come and gone, and those formative Industrial Revolution years had produced and improved the steam engine. Rails had been constructed across the country, and steam engines were pulling trains over railroads that tapped both the largest and smallest towns of the United States. Railroads held an almost exclusive franchise on intercity transportation. To maintain their image, railroads began to construct grand temples of transportation in major cities, each one seeking to outdo the other in size and grandeur. New York City got its colossal Pennsylvania Station in 1910 and Grand Central Station in 1913. In smaller cities, splendid edifices were also beginning to blossom in all shapes and sizes. In the South, Louisville had its Union Station in 1880, Montgomery's Union Station opened in 1897, Nashville secured its Union Station in 1900, Savannah's Union Station opened in 1902, and Knoxville's Southern Railway Station and Augusta's Union Station opened in 1903. Atlanta's Terminal Station was completed in 1905, Chattanooga and Birmingham's Terminal Station were opened for business in 1909, and Memphis Union Station opened in 1912.

Macon, however, was having serious problems securing a new union station. Although admittedly smaller than any of the aforementioned cities and towns, it had nothing to be ashamed of with the nearly 100 daily trains stopping at this city of less than 50,000 people, who had to be satisfied with the 1855 Union Depot and its equally embarrassing Southern Railway Fifth and Ocmulgee Streets station.

On September 28, 1912, Col. Robert L. Berner, prominent Macon attorney and former state senator, petitioned the Georgia Railroad Commission to require all passenger railroads entering Macon to erect an adequate station in the city. This brought about an immediate response from the railroads, when on Wednesday, February 5, 1913, Central of Georgia Railway vice president W.A. Winburn announced that plans had been formulated for the building of a lavish new station on Cherry Street that only needed the city's cooperation along with the state legislature to allow it to become reality. Streets at the station site had to be closed, along with others on the approaches to the station. This could be accomplished only by legislation. On May 27, 1913, additional good news came from Southern Railway vice president H.B. Spencer that the Southern Railway, Macon's second-largest train provider, had agreed to joint occupancy of the new station and would share in the cost of its construction. This was followed shortly after by the Georgia Southern & Florida Railway, which also agreed to share in the costs involved in building the new Terminal Station. It took close to an additional year, but on April 22, 1914, an announcement was made that a terminal company representing all railroads entering Macon would shortly be formed to allow for the building of the new station and its use by all companies then operating into Macon. By May 30, Central of Georgia, acting for the proposed terminal company, had New York architects already drawing up the plans and specifications for the new 13-acre station. On July 9, the Macon Terminal Company was created and was in official operation.

The architect chosen to design Macon Terminal Station was Alfred Fellheimer. Born in 1875, the Fellheimer was only 28 years old when he began working for the firm of Reed & Stem and served as chief architect for the building of New York City's fabulous Grand Central Station. His specialization in railroad architecture was why he was chosen to be the architect of Macon's masterpiece station just 12 years later. In time, he went on to design a number of other famed railroad stations, including in Buffalo and Erie. His work culminated in 1929 with the Art Deco gem he envisioned for Cincinnati's Union Terminal, which still stands.

On March 12, 1915, the Georgia Railroad Commission approved the general plans for Macon Terminal Station and instructed the Macon Terminal Company to submit its final plans no later than September 15. Additionally, it ordered that the station, its passenger platforms, tracks, and all approaches had to be completed within 12 months after the detailed plans and specifications were approved. This assured that Macon Terminal Station would be in operation by January 1917. Macon's long-standing dream would finally be realized. On December 1, 1916, the doors to Macon Terminal Station were thrown open to a more than elated Macon! On the same day, the doors were also thrown open in the station for a three-chair barbershop operated by H.L. Jenkins.

The new station's prominent personnel included W.F. Whipple, stationmaster; Andrew W. Staley, night stationmaster; E.P. Bonner, ticket agent; H.F. Cherry, baggage agent; R.L. Bateman, chief clerk to the stationmaster; Z.T. Rogers, A.G. Reddy, day train callers; H.L. Finney, night train caller; J.M. Lavender, J.C. Langston, R.I. Fletcher, and T.A. Ousley, gatekeepers; A.B. Burroughs, R.A. Lawton, L.O. Vann, and C.L. Roqueniore, baggage clerks; Parks Ousley and C.J. Vann, railway mail clerks; and J.T. Minor, US mail transfer clerk.

During Macon Terminal Station's tenure, numerous celebrities passed through its portals, not to mention the millions of regular passengers whose names will never be known, some of whom, like the many soldiers who went off to war, would never return. As for the trains that ventured through the terminal, besides the numerous local accommodation trains and even a few mixed trains that never warranted a specific name, the station saw a number of grand trains. These included Central of Georgia's *Nancy Hanks*, *Flamingo*, *Southland*, and *Dixie Flyer*. Southern Railway's name trains included the *Suwanee Limited*, *South Atlantic Limited*, *Florida Special*, *Sunbeam*, *Ponce de Leon*, *Royal Palm*, *New Royal Palm*, and the *Kansas City-Florida Special*. Also rating a name, although it was far from a streamliner, was GS&F's humble *Shoofly*, which daily plied the 152 miles between Macon and Valdosta.

The Right Way Magazine

ISSUED MONTHLY *by* CENTRAL *of* GEORGIA RAILWAY

SEPTEMBER   1921

ENTRANCE TO PASSENGER STATION, MACON, GA.

The September 1921 Central of Georgia's *The Right Way Magazine* featured Macon Terminal Station. Less than six years old, the station was already beginning to show some signs of aging. (Courtesy CGRHS.)

CENTRAL OF GEORGIA RAILWAY COMPANY
"THE RIGHT WAY"

PASSENGER TRAFFIC DEPARTMENT

Bulletin No. 3

OPENING OF NEW TERMINAL STATION, MACON, GA., DECEMBER 1, 1916

ALL AGENTS, SOLICITING REPRESENTATIVES,
CONDUCTORS, BAGGAGE AGENTS, AND OFFICIALS
OF CONNECTING LINES:

The new Terminal Station at Macon, Georgia, has been completed and effective at the hour of 9.00 O'Clock A.M. December 1, 1916, all passenger trains of the CENTRAL OF GEORGIA RAILWAY, will arrive at and depart therefrom. The following station officials will be prepared to handle such business as properly comes before them: W. F. Wippler, Stationmaster; E. P. Bonner, Ticket Agent; H. T. Cherry, General Baggage Agent.

The new terminal will be used by all railway lines entering Macon, viz:

> CENTRAL OF GEORGIA RAILWAY COMPANY
> GEORGIA SOUTHERN & FLORIDA RAILWAY
> SOUTHERN RAILWAY
> GEORGIA RAILROAD
> MACON & BIRMINGHAM RAILWAY
> MACON, DUBLIN & SAVANNAH RAILROAD

The trains of all of these railways will also enter and depart from the new station at and after 9.00 A.M. December 1: Except trains of Southern Railway, date to be announced later. Prior to that hour all trains will adhere to present arrangements.

Macon transfer coupons in tickets sold for trains scheduled to arrive at Macon after 9.00 A.M. on the date named, should be marked void except in tickets reading over Southern Railway from Macon.

The main entrance to the new terminal opens on Cherry street and is most conveniently located with respect to hotels, business houses and places of amusements.

It is desired that all possible publicity be given to the new facilities.

F. J. Robinson

SAVANNAH, GA., NOV. 27, 1916

General Passenger Agent.

Central of Georgia proudly announced with Bulletin No. 3 that Macon Terminal Station would open on December 1, 1916. It was an occasion that would be remembered by every Maconite. (Courtesy CGRHS.)

A stately, but seemingly empty, Terminal Station basks in the afternoon summer sun in June 1966. (Courtesy CGRHS, A.M. Langley Jr., photographer.)

Not much activity is apparent at Terminal Station in this June 1966 image. In five more years, there will be no movement whatsoever. (Courtesy CGRHS, A.M. Langley Jr., photographer.)

Taken sometime in early 1916, this is the only known photograph of Terminal Station's head house under construction. The station was ready for use in October 1916, but its opening was delayed by legal action taken by local residents over the Pine Street overpass, which was then under construction.

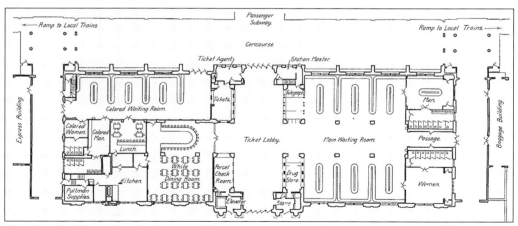

This detailed floor plan for Terminal Station appeared in *Railway Age* magazine. The spacious layout is easily discerned in this image. (Courtesy CGRHS.)

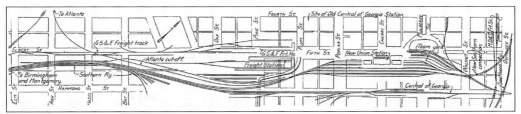

This sketch details the general layout of Terminal Station and nearby Macon Junction with the Atlanta cut-off. Note the crossing of the double-track freight and passenger lines. This image also appeared in *Railway Age* magazine. (Courtesy CGRHS.)

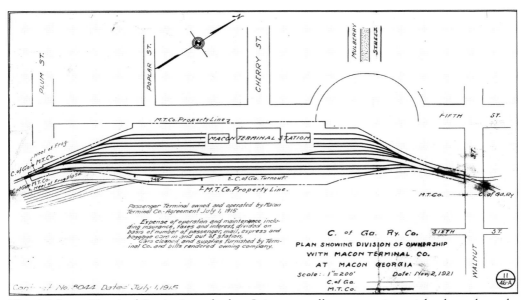

This is Macon Terminal Station's track plan. It is not totally correct, since eight through tracks were created instead of the originally planned six. (Courtesy CGRHS.)

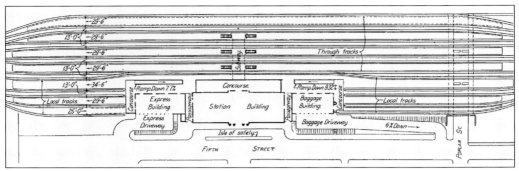

This Terminal Station track plan appeared in *Railway Age* magazine. It shows that only six through tracks were originally planned, but as indicated by the dotted lines, eight were constructed. (Courtesy CGRHS.)

This postcard from the 1920s shows a beautiful station alive with activity. The arched opening on the right provided a direct entrance to the checked baggage building.

Terminal Station is still under construction. The tracks have yet to be leveled, and the platforms have been built temporarily with wood. Concrete platforms could not be poured on the site until the eight-foot fill fully settled. (Courtesy Ed Mims, W.H. Mims Collection.)

This is the first of a series of images that show Macon Terminal Station from its main entrance to its back concourse and station platform area. They provide a good visual impression of the station's enormity and what it looked like when it was an operating station. Regrettably, the bulk of these photographs were captured after the station had already been closed and show the station in an obvious state of disrepair.

In the late 1940s, Terminal Station's grand main entrance is pictured with a small crowd of people milling around.

Terminal Station is pictured here in November 1971. Central of Georgia's *Nancy Hanks II* made its last run on April 30 of that year. At this point, it was anyone's guess what would become of the 1916 masterpiece. The station appears spotless; however, it was forlorn and abandoned and possibly headed for the scrap pile.

These photographs were taken on Sunday, June 11, 1972. The Schlitz trucks parked in front of what was once the station's Railway Express Building reveal that this wing was most likely leased for warehouse space.

This 1972 photograph of Macon Terminal Station shows the checked baggage building to the right of the head house. The station has been closed and awaits its destiny.

By the time of this October 1973 image, the station had been closed for over a year and a half. According to the banner, there is a Goodyear warehouse sale in progress.

In May 1973, the boarded up former checked baggage building tells the story of a station no longer needed. No one would have believed that the station was destined for better times.

Seen here in June 1974, the six percent ramp provided direct access to the checked baggage building. Heavy luggage and trunks could be brought directly to checking without having to carry them through the station.

Here, Terminal Station has yet to open. The brand-new waiting room is primed for its first guests, due to arrive on December 1, 1916. This photograph was taken from the ticket lobby, looking toward the waiting room. Telephone and telegraph offices were in the enclosed area to the left, while a drugstore occupied the right enclosed area. This image appeared in a souvenir brochure that the railroads issued on the occasion of Terminal Station's opening. (Courtesy Jim Goolsby.)

The curt "keep out" sign warns trespassers to stay away; however, there is no one to caution in this view, which was taken long after Terminal Station had been padlocked.

This June 11, 1972, photograph was taken just inside the main entrance. The lights are off, the trains are no more, and no one passes through these portals rushing to catch a train.

This image looks toward the concourse area. The station is closed, and no one will need to check train times on the clock above the doors.

On June 11, 1972, only the sun provides any light in an otherwise dark and barren station. The benches have been pushed to the side in an orderly fashion, in contrast to some other images of the interior showing them in disarray and blocking the entrance.

In 1916, not everyone was welcome to enter Macon Terminal Station through the main entrance. African Americans had a separate entrance, waiting room, and eating facilities.

Emptiness exists around the once vibrant ticket booth, pictured above in 1969 and below in September 1970. Although Terminal Station did not officially close until 1971, not many people were interested in what few trains remained. This was in sharp contrast to what the *Macon Telegraph* reported on May 6, 1923, when some 4,300 passengers were passing through Terminal Station daily.

The trains are no more, and so the passengers are no more. This is what the inside of the ticket booth looked like when it was all over. Once, up to seven employees worked here.

The oak benches sit empty, as passengers no longer crowd the station. It is after April 1971, and Macon Terminal Station is no longer operating.

The photograph above shows the waiting room just after the station closed in 1971. The water fountain was still in place, and the station was still in good repair. Below, over two years later, the water fountain is gone and rainwater from the leaking roof has left stains on the floor. The open door led to the former women's waiting room.

The door to the left above led to
a no-longer-needed men's room,
seen in a closer view at right.

This photograph from April 1973 shows a section of what was once the black lunchroom. Debris has been allowed to pile up everywhere.

To accommodate the tens of thousands of servicemen and women of Camp Wheeler, the United Service Organizations (USO) built a bar in Terminal Station. Needless to say, it became a beehive of activity.

Central of Georgia Locomotive No. 485 heads a heavy *Dixie Limited* on its way to Atlanta and points north. The photograph, taken just outside Macon, dates to sometime in the 1940s or 1950s.

This is what Macon Terminal Station was once all about—passengers! A large load of humanity is preparing to catch the northbound *Nancy Hanks II* on its way to Atlanta in the 1960s.

In 1973, beautiful Terminal Station had been closed two years, but one would never know it from this image.

These doors, which lead from the head house into the concourse area, are closed, and no one will be opening them. It is June 11, 1972, and the station has been closed over a year.

This is the passageway that led
to the subway area beneath the
platform tracks. Eight through tracks
could be reached from this point.

June 1969 finds the head house's
doors to the concourse area bolted
open, in the hope of helping
passengers catch their train. There
will be few riders to speak of.

This image shows the concourse area between the Terminal Station's head house, on the right, and the ramp leading to the tracks and platforms. On this late day in 1970, only a few people can be seen on the concourse. The purpose of the fenced-in cage at left is unknown.

It is now June 1972. The station has been closed, and the lights are off. A bleak future seems destined for the abandoned station.

The station is desolate; there is not a soul in sight. The trains are no more, as is obvious from the abandoned concourse.

This image's photographer and the exact date it was taken will probably never be known. What is known is that this is the northbound Central of Georgia *Flamingo*, headed for Atlanta and eventually Cincinnati, Ohio, and that the photograph was taken in 1947 or 1948. Assuming the train is running on schedule, the time would be after 4:00 in the afternoon. To travel between the train's two destinations, Jacksonville and Cincinnati, required three separate railroads: the Atlantic Coast Line from Jacksonville to Albany, Georgia; the Central of Georgia to Atlanta; and the Louisville & Nashville to reach Cincinnati. The many headend cars that the train is pulling

give evidence that the *Flamingo* was the "workhorse" train of this route. At this late date, Macon Terminal Station was virtually empty, in stark contrast to 1916 when as many as 10 trains could be in the station at any given time. Looking closely, the engineer is leaning out of his window to watch the locomotive's drivers and to apply sand to the rails to avoid a bad slip as he accelerates the heavy train out of Macon Terminal Station. Additionally, note the railroad post office clerk, dining car chief, and the train's conductor standing in their cars' doorways. (Courtesy Ed Mims, W.H. Mims Collection.)

These two images, taken of the same spot, show the back of Terminal Station's entrance, looking toward the doors that connect to the concourse. The photograph at left was taken in 1959 when the station was near its life's end but still in use. The image below is from 1972, after the station had closed. Note the missing clock in the lower image. It is possible that some relic hunter snatched it up.

This is one of Hubert Hawthorne's rare images showing the Terminal Station concourse, looking east toward the Railway Express Building. The right entrance allowed access to the five stub-end passenger loading tracks, located at that end of the 7.7 percent up ramp, while the left door gave direct access to the street. The doors to the left grant access to the main station head house and lobby. Not visible between the first concrete columns, just beyond these doors, is the entrance that led to the black waiting room. One of the station's platforms can be seen to the right, just outside the station's covered concourse area. (Courtesy Ed Mims, H. Hawthorne Collection.)

This view again highlights the spacious Terminal Station concourse. This photograph was taken in 1916 before the station opened. It shows the calm before the storm. (Courtesy Ed Mims, H. Hawthorne Collection.)

In February 1976, Terminal Station is closed, and its umbrella sheds and tracks have been removed. The station awaits its fate.

This is a 1955 view of several locomotives outside Macon's sprawling Central of Georgia repair shops. This was a publicity photograph taken by the railroad to show off its fleet of modern equipment.

Through these doors and down the steps brought passengers to the subway beneath the eight through tracks in Macon Terminal. In this June 1972 scene, the passengers are long gone.

The doors leading to the tunnel beneath the platform tracks have been boarded up in this June 22, 1972, photograph. Plaster has fallen or been pulled off the bricks, and water from the leaking roof appears to have pooled along the base of the wall.

These are the steps that led from the concourse to the subway area beneath the passenger platform waiting area. These narrow and steep stairs might have been the one minor negative point in the station's design.

The once vibrant subway, teeming with people beneath the tracks, is anything but that in this 1963 scene. The end is now not far off.

This is a view of the subway area in better times. The obvious gloom is still evident in this late scene. The steps at left led to trainside. This was one of only two places where passengers had to use steps to reach their destination.

Here, Terminal Station is closed. This bleak view captures the back of the station and shows the ramp toward the head house. The handrail is bent from years of use.

Just prior to Macon Terminal Station's opening, the railroads issued a brochure boasting about it. Included was this image of a perfectly spotless concourse area, proudly anticipating its first passengers.

This is yet another image of the backside of Terminal Station after it was closed and the tracks and platforms had been removed. It is May 1973, and a trainload of railroad fans from Atlanta have ridden behind the Savannah & Atlanta steam locomotive No. 750 into Macon. The train is now beginning its return trip to the Georgia capital. (Courtesy Lloyd Neal.)

This photograph was taken on the first platform at Track No. 1, just behind the station. No one would guess from this scene that the station had already been closed.

The five stub tracks that adorned Terminal Station on either side of the station were reached via this ramp, as well as the concourse and head house. The base is dark. It is June 1972, and the trains are no more.

The man visible in both these images may be the same person, and it is possible that both photographs were taken at the same time. The one above has a date of July 1970. Both were taken behind the head house and show an empty Track No. 1.

Tracks Nos. 2 and 3 are devoid of any activity as Macon Terminal Station awaits it final outcome. The "caution" sign on the edge of the shed was intended for railroaders hanging onto the outside of a car while switching in the station, to make them aware that there was insufficient clearance beyond that point.

Heavy-duty equipment occupies what were once train tracks and station platforms. It is December 19, 1973. These machines are destroying what took so many years to perfect.

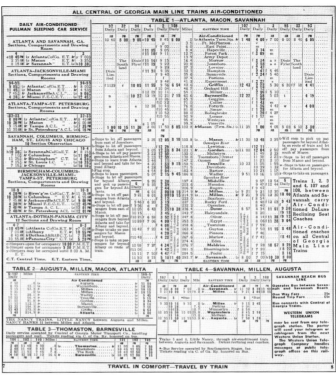

There had been a reduction in service by April 24, 1949. Nonetheless, Macon was still going strong with six daily services via Central of Georgia to Atlanta and three to Savannah. Southern Railway's Atlanta service also included four additional Atlanta round trips. Service was still available to Athens, and even mixed-train service could be had to Porterdale, Georgia. (Both, CGRHS.)

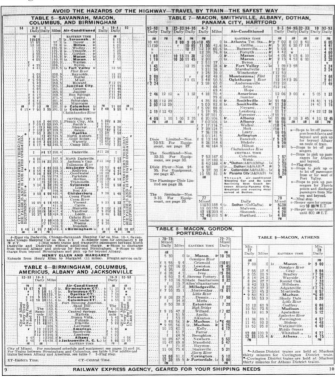

Southern Railway was the second-largest provider of Macon train service. Its Midwest-to-Florida service was held down by its two major-name trains, the *Royal Palm* and the *Ponce de Leon*. It was not uncommon for these trains, as well as Central of Georgia's Florida-bound trains, to operate in two or more sections, greatly increasing the traffic volume into Terminal Station. (Courtesy Marvin Clemons.)

Locomotive No. 163 began its life in 1904 as Baldwin-built No. 1063. In 1925, it became No. 163 and was made the Terminal Station shed engine, used exclusively in and around the station. As needed, it switched Pullman, dining, and chair cars from trains entering Macon. (Courtesy CGRHS.)

As it had done for years, MD&S Train No. 18 has just arrived at 2:45 p.m. from Vidalia. This time, it will not be returning. It is December 31, 1949, and the lack of patronage has brought about its demise.

On December 31, 1949, engineer J.F. Heyser, a 41-year MD&S veteran, poses for his portrait on the last day he will serve as engineer for Passenger Train No. 17 to Vidalia. Starting the following day, he will command a freight train.

MD&S Train No. 17 has left Terminal Station and has just crossed the Ocmulgee River. It is speeding along to Vidalia for the last time.

Exactly where this photograph was taken is unknown. It shows the final MD&S train out of Macon to Vidalia on December 31, 1949.

With a good photographer, even a local accommodation train, such as the MD&S seen here, can look great. Hugh Comer captured Train No. 18 as it pranced 30 miles south of Macon at Danville, Georgia, in December 1945. (Courtesy Marvin Clemons.)

The *Dixie Limited* is just on the outskirts of Macon, near Wesleyan College, in this 1940s image. Being pulled by Central of Georgia No. 485, the train is speeding inbound from Atlanta and northern points and is on its way to Florida destinations. (Courtesy Ed Mims, W.H. Mims Collection.)

On December 18, 1947, Macon Terminal was still a busy station, and a lot of people saw this Macon advertisement. (Courtesy CGRHS.)

On July 11, 1947, the new *Nancy Hanks II* is parked in Macon Terminal, where it is being paraded prior to going into revenue service on July 17. The train was a hit for a while, but after just 24 years, patronage dwindled to the point that it was no longer worthwhile. (Courtesy CGRHS.)

The northbound *Flamingo* is ready to depart in December 1960. It is being led by a Central of Georgia RS-3. (Courtesy CGRHS, Howard Robins, photographer.)

It is July 17, 1948, one year to the day that the new *Nancy Hanks II* was placed in revenue service. Always seeking to publicize its passenger trains, the Central of Georgia brought in photographers to celebrate the anniversary. (Courtesy CGRHS.)

Arriving from Atlanta, Central of Georgia Train No. 1 is just outside Macon Terminal Station. An E7 heads the train in this undated scene. (Courtesy CGRHS.)

The *Nancy Hanks* is just in from Savannah on Track No. 8 in 1951. A small handful of people queue up to board the Atlanta-bound train. The turnout in the foreground leads to the Terminal Station's coach yard, where coaches, diners, and Pullman cars were stored. (Courtesy CGRHS.)

These c. 1960 photographs show Train No. 17, the northbound *Flamingo*, preparing to depart Macon Terminal Station on a rainy day. (Both, courtesy CGRHS, Howard Robins, photographer.)

Above, the *Flamingo* waits its turn to pull out for Atlanta. Not too many people are there to witness its departure. Below, on a hot day in August 1958, the *Flamingo* has come in on Track No. 7. (Both, courtesy Ed Mims.)

Train No. 18 is on its way to Atlanta and points north. The Central of Georgia paint scheme of green and yellow began to be used in January 1959. Here, the train's crew exchanges idle talk while the mail and baggage are unloaded. (Courtesy CGRHS, Howard Robins, photographer.)

Though similar to the image above, this photograph shows very few passengers, which explains why Train No. 18, the *Flamingo*, would be making its last run on this day, June 30, 1963. (Courtesy CGRHS, Howard Robins, photographer.)

In this 1960 photograph, three trains are at Macon Terminal Station. A Central of Georgia Alco RS-3 (left) leads the *Flamingo*, and the Southern PA-3 (center) leads its *Ponce de Leon*. The Central of Georgia 806 EMD (right) is believed to have been left for service on the *Nancy Hanks II*. (Courtesy CGRHS, Howard Robins, photographer.)

It is April 30, 1971. A Southern FP7 heads the final *Nancy Hanks II* out of Macon. This was the last train to Atlanta. (Courtesy CGRHS, A.M. Langley Jr., photographer.)

The *Flamingo* is seen again in Macon Terminal Station. Train No. 17 was popular with railfans, and numerous photographs were taken of it. (Courtesy CGRHS, Howard Robins, photographer.)

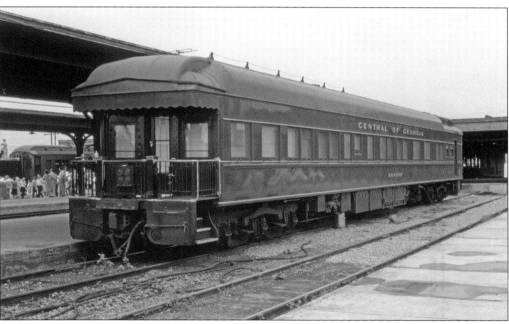

A Central of Georgia office car sits on one of Macon Terminal Station's 10 stub tracks in 1966. This car was built in 1927 as the *Marco Polo* and used as a business car by the Pullman Company. Pres. Franklin D. Roosevelt used the car extensively from 1933 to 1940. In 1944, the Central of Georgia purchased the car and changed its name to *Savannah*. In the late 1970s, it was leased by the Chattanooga Choo Choo, and it was purchased by the Southern Railway in 1983 and returned to Washington, DC. (Courtesy CGRHS, Howard Robins, photographer.)

This image is from a souvenir brochure that the railroads issued when Terminal Station opened in 1916. By today's printing standards, the image makes the station appear dull. Nonetheless, for that era, the brochure did its job, and Maconites were elated to read about the new station they had been waiting over 30 years for. (Courtesy Jim Goolsby.)

Wesleyan College in Macon once had its own Central of Georgia station, giving students easy access to trains when they traveled on break. With the abandonment of passenger service, the station is shown here being demolished.

ARRIVING TRAINS				DEPARTING TRAINS			
SOUTHERN RAILWAY							
TRAIN NO.	FROM	DUE TO ARRIVE	EXPECTED TO ARRIVE	TRAIN NO.	TO	DUE TO DEPART	EXPECTED TO DEPART
CENTRAL OF GEORGIA							
TRAIN NO.	FROM	DUE TO ARRIVE	EXPECTED TO ARRIVE	TRAIN NO.	TO	DUE TO DEPART	EXPECTED TO DEPART
7	SAVANNAH	7.45 AM	ON TIME	7	ATLANTA	7.30 AM	ON TIME
8	ATLANTA	8.05 PM	ON TIME		SAVANNAH	8.15 PM	ON TIME
GEORGIA R.R.							
TRAIN NO.	FROM	DUE TO ARRIVE	EXPECTED TO ARRIVE	TRAIN NO.	TO	DUE TO DEPART	EXPECTED TO DEPART
24	AUGUSTA				AUGUSTA		

Photographer Richard Stewart captured Terminal Station's bulletin board in August 1966. This is a far cry from the nearly 100 daily arrivals and departures in 1916. (Courtesy CGRHS.)

When Southern Railway assumed control of the Central of Georgia on June 17, 1963, the Central's locomotives were painted in Southern's austere black-and-white color scheme. Here, two railroad employees stand beside the northbound *Nancy Hanks II.*

This splendid photograph was taken in August 1966. Photographer Richard Stewart is riding into Macon Terminal on the northbound *Nancy Hanks II*. What appears to be an empty station

awaits the Atlanta-bound train's arrival. With the train's passing in less than five years, the station would have no reason to remain in existence. (Courtesy CGRHS.)

These two photographs were both taken on the same day in August 1966. In just five more years, the *Nancy Hanks*, seen here, would be no more. The weeds tell of a station dying a slow and agonizing death. Below, a small crowd is boarding in the background. (Both, courtesy CGRHS, Richard Stewart, photographer.)

The *Nancy* is snaking into Terminal Station from Savannah in August 1966. In less than five years, the train will cease operation. (Courtesy CGRHS, Richard Stewart, photographer.)

Here is another April 30, 1971, image of the *Nancy*'s last trip out of Terminal Station. Note the employees conversing on the right. One man appears to be holding a toolbox and lunch bag. (Courtesy CGRHS, A.M. Langley Jr., photographer.)

ARRIVES	DEPARTS	TRAIN NUMBER AND NAME	FROM	TO	RAILROAD
1:00 AM	1:05 AM	# 33-18 THE SOUTHLAND	ATLANTA	VALDOSTA	CofG-GS&F
1:10 AM		# 4	MONTGOMERY		CofG
1:20 AM		# 12	MONTGOMERY		CofG
1:25 AM	1:45 AM	# 4	ATLANTA	SAVANNAH	CofG
1:40 AM	1:45 AM	#11 THE ROYAL PALM	CINCINNATI	JACKSONVILLE	SOUTHERN
2:30 AM		# 8	ATLANTA		CofG
	2:50 AM	# 3		FORT VALLEY	CofG
2:30 AM	2:55 AM	# 3	SAVANNAH	ATLANTA	CofG
	2:55 AM	# 11		MONTGOMERY	CofG
2:55 AM	3:00 AM	# 8 KANSAS CITY-FLORIDA SPECIAL	JACKSONVILLE	KANSAS CITY	SOUTHERN
3:40 AM	3:45 AM	# 12 THE ROYAL PALM	JACKSONVILLE	CINCINNATI	SOUTHERN
3:53 AM	3:58 AM	# 32 THE SOUTHLAND	JACKSONVILLE	CINCINNATI	GS&F-CofG
4:25 AM	4:30 AM	# 94 THE DIXIE FLYER	JACKSONVILLE	CHICAGO	GS&F-CofG
4:50 AM		# 10	JACKSONVILLE		GS&F
	5:00 AM	# 30		CAMEK, GA	GEORGIA
	6:25 AM	# 32		GORDON, GA	CofG
	7:05 AM	# 43		LAGRANGE, GA	M&B
	7:30 AM	# 11		ATLANTA	CofG
	7:30 AM	# 13		ATHENS, GA	CofG
	7:30 AM	# 28		ATLANTA	SOUTHERN
9:25 AM		# 30	HAZELHURST, GA		SOUTHERN
9:30 AM		# 8	SMITHVILLE, GA		CofG
9:45 AM		# 21	MILLEN, GA		CofG
10:50 AM	10:55 AM	# 27	ATLANTA	BRUNSWICK	SOUTHERN
10:50 AM		# 19	VIDALIA, GA		MD&S
10:50 AM		# 6	VALDOSTA		GS&F
11:00 AM		# 14	ATHENS, GA		CofG
11:00 AM		# 40	LAGRANGE,GA		M&B
	11:10 AM	# 9		ATLANTA	CofG
11:15 AM		# 31	CAMEK, GA		GEORGIA
	11:20 AM	# 1		JACKSONVILLE	GS&F
	11:40 AM	# 5		MONTGOMERY	CofG
12:35 PM	12:40 PM	# 7 KANSAS CITY-FLORIDA SPECIAL	KANSAS CITY	JACKSONVILLE	SOUTHERN
	1:00 PM	# 1		FORT VALLEY	CofG
12:55 PM	1:30 PM	# 1	SAVANNAH	ATLANTA	CofG
2:25 PM	2:30 PM	# 10 THE FLORIDA SPECIAL	JACKSONVILLE	CINCINNATI	SOUTHERN
2:30 PM	2:35 PM	# 9 THE FLORIDA SPECIAL	CINCINNATI	JACKSONVILLE	SOUTHERN
	3:20 PM	# 20		SAVANNAH	MD&S
3:40 PM	5:00 PM	# 10-22	ATLANTA	MONTGOMERY	CofG
	4:10 PM	# 5		TIFTON, GA	GS&F
	4:15 PM	# 3		HAZELHURST	SOUTHERN
4:25 PM		# 26			GS&F
	4:45 PM	# 34		CAMEK, GA	GEORGIA
	4:45 PM	# 41		LAGRANGE, GA	M&B
4:35 PM	4:50 PM	# 26	JACKSONVILLE	ATLANTA	SOUTHERN
4:40 PM		# 6	MONTGOMERY		CofG
4:50 PM		# 2	SMITHVILLE, GA		CofG
	4:50 PM	# 23		ATHENS, GA	CofG
	5:00 PM	# 15		ATLANTA	CofG
	5:00 PM	# 7		MONTGOMERY	CofG
7:20 PM		# 12		ATLANTA	CofG
8:25 PM		# 42	LAGRANGE,GA		M&B
8:30 PM		# 29	ATLANTA		SOUTHERN
8:40 PM		# 24	ATHENS, GA		CofG
9:40 PM		# 17	GORDON, GA		CofG
10:40 PM		# 35	CAMEK, GA		GEORGIA
	11:00 PM	# 3		JACKSONVILLE	GS&F
11:22 PM	11:32 PM	# 94 THE DIXIE FLYER	CHICAGO	JACKSONVILLE	CofG-GS&F

This is another image of the *Nancy*'s last day of operation. It is taking on the necessary water for the remaining distance to Atlanta. (Courtesy CGRHS, A.M. Langley Jr., photographer.)

This is a typical 24-hour lineup at Macon Terminal Station during the 1920s. At certain times of the day, multiple trains were bunched in the station. In those days, trains often ran in two or even three sections.

Just outside of Macon Terminal, the Central of Georgia mainline took trains over this high overhead trestle. The amazing image above was captured by A.M. Langley Jr. while riding the *Nancy* on April 30, 1971, while the photograph below was taken at about the same location by Richard Stewart in August 1966. (Above, courtesy A.M. Langley Jr.; below, courtesy Richard Stewart.)

This beautiful March 5, 1949, photograph was taken on the same Vineville trestle as the previous images. It captures Train No. 93, the *Dixie Limited*, being led by Mountain-type Locomotive No.

490 on its way to Atlanta. (Courtesy CGRHS, W.T. Reid, photographer.)

Ben Roberts captured the amazing image above from inside the locomotive. The train is nearing the Vineville trestle, which is depicted in the previous images. Rest assured, the engineer is taking it slow and easy as he negotiates this turn. The photograph below was taken by A.M. Langley Jr. on April 30, 1971, the *Nancy's* last day. (Above, courtesy Ben Roberts; below, courtesy A.M. Langley Jr.)

Pictured in 1948, dispatchers operate the Centralized Traffic Control machine in Macon Terminal Station. The individual above is unidentified; Fred C. Laing is seen below. (Courtesy CGRHS.)

SEPTEMBER, 1953

Railroaders at Work
Leverman

Operator-leverman Levarne (above) and J. Henry Wilson (left) operate the 112-lever interlocking machine at Macon Junction. Here, double tracks from the Albany District cross over a double-track freight line serving Central of Georgia's West Yard and lead into Macon Terminal Station. (Courtesy CGRHS.)

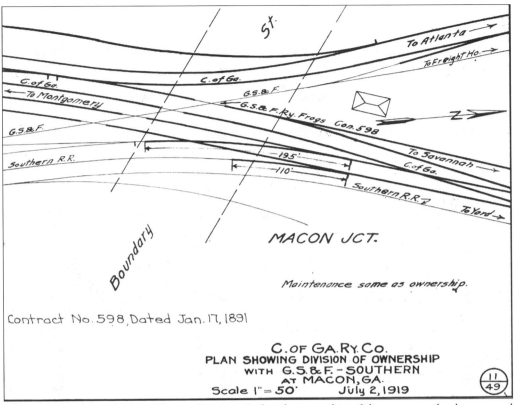

This diagram shows the busy Macon Junction. It details ownership of the many tracks that crossed that point. The Central of Georgia tracks to the left pass West Yard, which continues as the Albany District to Fort Valley, where trains branch off to either Columbus or Albany and other points west. Tracks to the right pass by Terminal Station and then continue east to Savannah. Trains from Atlanta enter the junction from the upper right. (Courtesy CGRHS.)

Central of Georgia 2-8-0 No. 505 heads an eastbound freight train through Macon Junction around 1940. The train is just to the west of Terminal Station, which it will pass very shortly. West Yard is out of view immediately behind the train. (Courtesy CGRHS.)

The location of this tower is yet to be positively determined. It is believed to be the important Macon Junction Tower that was just outside Terminal Station.

This view looks north toward Terminal Station and downtown Macon. It is August 1971, and the station has been closed for several months. The tracks that would have led into the station have been removed.

This scene is just outside Terminal Station, which can be discerned in the background. The date is October 1974, and Terminal Station has been closed for three years already.

Prior to commencing regular service on July 17, 1947, the new *Nancy Hanks II* is on parade in Macon Terminal Station on July 9.

When designing Macon Terminal Station, New York architect Alfred Fellheimer was inspired by previous stations. He modeled the exterior after Union Station in Washington, DC (above), which he had helped to create. The interior borrowed many features from Fellheimer's 1914 Union Station in Utica, New York (below). The similarities of both can be seen here. (Above, courtesy Library of Congress; below, courtesy Oneida County History Center.)

This aerial photograph captures Terminal Station to the left. Among other things, it shows the railroad bridge across the Ocmulgee River at far right. (Courtesy CGRHS.)

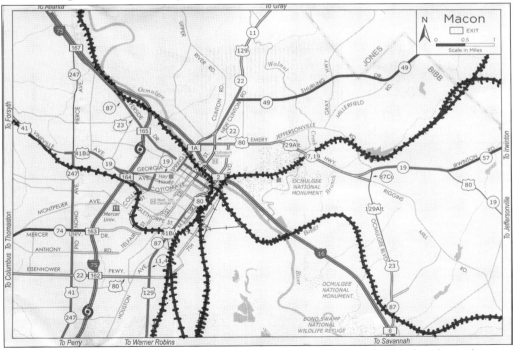

This map details the many railroads that made Macon an important rail hub. Like spokes in a wheel, lines stretched to Atlanta, Savannah, Columbus, Albany, Valdosta, Jacksonville, Brunswick, Athens, and even smaller towns, such as Camak, Vidalia, and LaGrange. Major cities could be reached directly, and by connection, virtually any town in America or Canada.

AGENT'S STAMP	Seat No. *51* Car No. A- **2**
	Train No. 107 Date_____19____
MAY =3'71	Time ____10:50 A.M._____
3 MACON, GA. 3	From ____MACON, GA._____
	To _____ATLANTA, GA._____

has been reserved in the name of or ticket number shown below for use on date indicated by stamp. Please show this card when boarding train and retain it as identification. If you cancel trip please notify agent at once. Not good for passage.

RESERVATION ONLY FOR DATE STAMPED

THIS IS A ONE-WAY RESERVATION ONLY. SEPARATE RESERVATION MUST BE MADE FOR RETURN TRIP. (See Reverse)

Central of Georgia Railway Co. _____361_____

Form RS-5   NAME OR TICKET NUMBER

Lloyd Neal rode the *Nancy Hanks* on April 3, 1971. Shown here is the reservation confirmation he secured from the ticket agent. Note that, by mistake, the agent advanced the ticket dater to May 3, which would have been several days after the *Nancy* was discontinued on April 30, 1971. (Courtesy Lloyd Neal.)

It is July 1, 1972. The last passenger train has left Terminal Station. Here, the station is being visited by the *Georgia Peach Special* excursion train from Atlanta. It has brought in a number of railroad buffs to tour the abandoned facility. (Courtesy CGRHS, A.M. Langley Jr., photographer.)

Macon's sprawling repair facility, built in 1909, could repair 25 locomotives simultaneously and had a 22-stall roundhouse, as well as machine, blacksmith, and boiler shops. (Courtesy Ed Mims.)

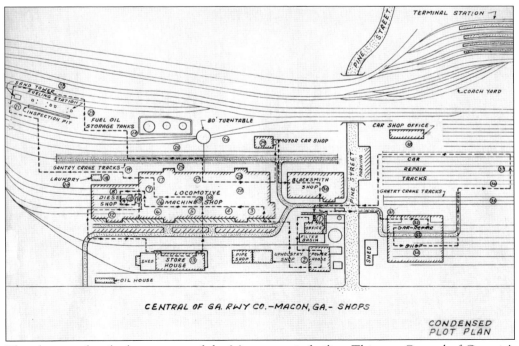

This drawing details the vastness of the Macon repair facility. This was Central of Georgia's primary repair facility. (Courtesy Ed Mims.)

This February 11, 1947, photograph was taken from the roof of Terminal Station. The sprawling Macon repair facility and Terminal Station's coach yard are visible. (Courtesy CGRHS.)

Captured shortly after the Macon repair facility opened in 1909, this view shows the locomotive repair shop. Note the small locomotives of the era as compared to the diesel giants of today. (Courtesy Ed Mims.)

The erecting bay section of the vast Macon Central of Georgia repair facility is seen in 1920. (Courtesy Ed Mims.)

This aerial view shows the large Central of Georgia repair facility. Some of Macon Terminal Station's platforms are visible at lower right. (Courtesy Ed Mims.)

This is yet another scene inside the repair facility. This picture captures the planing mill. This mill was needed primarily to repair floors and the linings of boxcars. (Courtesy Ed Mims.)

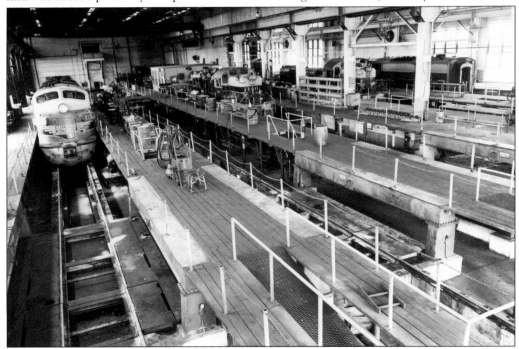

This 1953 image shows the diesel repair shop, which was relatively new at that time. Steam engines were being phased out from the railroad.

Passenger trains no longer serve Macon, but freight trains, for which the railroads were initially built, continue to pass daily through the city. In 1966, Southern Railway opened a $12 million hump yard in the city. Some 10,000 train cars pass through the yard weekly, and some 300 employees labor around the clock at the facility, dispatching trains to seven major points—Atlanta, Jacksonville, Savannah, Augusta, Albany, Columbus, and Brunswick.

Southern Railway's Brosnan Yard has 50 classification tracks. As a car approaches the crest of the hump, the conductor checks its number against the switch list and punches a button labeled with the number of the designated track onto which the car is to move. This button activates a computer, which then has complete control and guides the car through retarders that control its speed until it gently couples with another car on the proper track.

This is the control room for Southern's Brosnan Yards. The dispatcher is keeping a close eye on the operation. This image was captured in 1967, shortly after the new facility opened.

Closed-circuit television receivers in the Brosnan Yard Office monitor the movement of all inbound trains. Here, an office clerk reads each car's identification number into a recording machine. Later, the recording will be used to prepare a switch list.

Five

Today's Macon
Terminal Station

On April 30, 1971, Macon Terminal Station was padlocked. An article in the November 1977 *Preservation News* said it all: "Is Macon's Terminal Terminal?" Unlike other cities, whose colorful stations were unceremoniously reduced to memories, the City of Macon, through Mayor Buck Melton, purchased the striking, but in terrible condition, edifice in 1977 for only $150,000 through the city's Urban Development Authority. The city also explored the possibility of tearing the building down and constructing a new office and shopping center on the site. On July 29, 1982, however, the city reached an agreement with Georgia Power Company to purchase the station for $400,000 for use as its Middle Georgia headquarters. Georgia Power then began an extensive renovation program after employing the architectural firm of Dunwoody Beeland & Henderson to do the work. Architect Eugene Cox Dunwoody of that firm was a grandson of W.E. Dunwoody, who in 1913 was the president of the Macon Chamber of Commerce that recommended and substantiated the need for the new Terminal Station facility. Some $4 million were expended on renovating the second and third floors, as well as making structural repairs to the building to bring it up to modern standards. Georgia Power Company thereafter occupied the structure in 1984. Beginning in the mid-1990s, however, Georgia Power's operations were transferred to Atlanta and other sites, and once again, the building's future was in peril. The City of Macon, under the leadership of Mayor C. Jack Ellis's administration, once again came to the rescue on August 26, 2002, by repurchasing the station as part of a $6.7 million federal grant that called for major renovations of the station and the building of a Macon Transit Authority (MTA) bus transfer station on the site. Studies were undertaken to convert the building into an intermodal transportation facility. In 2005, the City of Macon secured an over $5 million Federal Transportation Grant to commence Phase I of the intermodal plan. Chris R. Sheridan & Company, working for NewTown Macon, which was contracted to manage the building, spent a year renovating the terminal. The renovations were completed in 2010. At that time, the MTA relocated its administrative offices to the main floor of the terminal and also located its Central Transfer Station to the site, as had been envisioned. In 2012, an attempt was made to transfer ownership of the property directly to the transit authority, but the proposal failed when it met stiff opposition from the Macon City Council. The fact was, however, that if the building's operational costs of mostly maintenance and utilities were to exceed rent paid by the tenants, the transit authority would not have been able to get the deficit covered by its federal subsidy unless the authority owned the building outright. In addition, federal officials would not consider any transportation grants that might help improve the building unless the authority had complete ownership. In July 2014, the city realized this, and when voted on for the second time, city council allowed the station to be officially transferred to the Macon-Bibb County Transit Authority, which was finalized in 2015. At this writing, the MTA manages the station's tenants and special events at the station. Today, the station is home to the Macon Transit Authority, and from its Central Transfer Station at Terminal Station, some 10 transit routes are dispatched throughout the city on a regular daily schedule. In addition, Macon's IT Department, the Macon Police Department's Youth & Intervention Unit, the Department of Economic and Community Development, the Macon-Bibb Office of Workforce Development, and Macon-Bibb County Planning and Zoning are located on the station's third floor. In what was once the railway express portion of the building, the Georgia Department of Driver Services has located an office. For a time, Terminal Station was also the site for the US Census Bureau 2010 Census.

Terminal Station's 1,000-foot-long platforms, its accompanying umbrella sheds, and 18 passenger loading tracks no longer exist. However, Macon Terminal Station's head house, described as downtown's "Crown Jewel," has been spared and is still in use, albeit in a different manner for which it was initially created. Today, besides housing the Macon Transit Authority executive offices and Central Transfer Station, along with various other offices, the station's primary attraction is its 14,000-square-foot beautifully restored lobby with original marble, gilt molding, and wooden benches. This has become a place for special occasions like weddings, receptions, parties, and fundraisers.

For some time, there has been talk calling for the reinstitution of passenger rail transportation between Macon and Atlanta. The use of Macon Terminal Station as the terminus has been seriously suggested. Should that become reality, once again, the station would serve its original purpose. This is not the first time train service through the terminal has been envisioned, however. As early as 1990, Amtrak did a study to consider reviving the *Floridian* route, which would have brought it through Macon. The proposal called for the train to utilize the old L&N *Dixie Route* through Nashville and Chattanooga as far as Dalton, Georgia. There, the train would have switched over to Southern Railway tracks to avoid the busy L&N line into Atlanta and continue through Macon to Vienna, Georgia. At that point, the old ex-Alabama, Birmingham & Coast Railway line is less than one mile away from the Southern (Georgia Southern & Florida) right-of-way, and a connection could have been made through the cotton fields to reach the Jacksonville terminus. Nothing, however, developed past the planning stages.

In the meantime, with or without trains, beautiful Macon Terminal Station survives, and at this writing, it appears to have a glorious future still ahead!

It can probably be said without hesitation that today's restored Terminal Station is as handsome as it was the day it opened on December 1, 1916. Here, the head house glistens in the afternoon sun. (Courtesy Robert M. Craig, photographer.)

The waiting room's beautifully restored ceiling, marble walls, and wooden benches are captured in this January 16, 2014, image. Although the station is once again often filled with people for special events like weddings, could the benches talk, they would probably wish to have the railroad passengers back. (Courtesy Robert M. Craig, photographer.)

This photograph shows Terminal Station's main entrance on Cherry Street. To the left is the waiting room. To the right was once the checked baggage room. Note the high-arched groin-vaulted roof with its gilt molding, and the marble walls and flooring. (Courtesy Robert M. Craig, photographer.)

In this January 16, 2014, view, a portion of the spacious waiting room is seen. When Terminal Station was in peak operation from its opening to World War II, it would rarely have been this empty. (Courtesy Robert M. Craig, photographer.)

With the Cherry Street entrance in view, many renovations can be seen that restored Terminal Station to its original grandeur. Note the elaborate groined vaults forming the ceiling, complemented with gilt molding, as well as the original lamp hanging just as it did when the station opened in 1916. (Courtesy Robert M. Craig, photographer.)

The grandeur and craftsmanship that went into Terminal Station is vividly captured in these 2014 images of the restored station. At left is an interesting stairway leading to the second floor. Below, note the simple beauty of the handrails. The railings are not of standard cast iron but instead are, as one *Macon Telegraph* reporter wrote, "a lyrical composition of the iron monger's art." (Both, courtesy Robert M. Craig, photographer.)

This photograph, taken on January 16, 2014, shows the back side of the station's entrance, heading toward the concourse and subway area beneath the platform tracks. (Courtesy Robert M. Craig, photographer.)

Taken near the station's Cherry Street entrance, this photograph not only provides a glimpse of the waiting room area, but also a view of the renovated second story. Today, the second story houses the offices of the Macon Business Development Department, while the Macon–Bibb County Planning and Zoning Department has recently relocated to the third floor. (Courtesy Robert M. Craig, photographer.)

This is the downtown Central Transfer Station that has been built in front of what once was Terminal Station's checked baggage building. A portion of Terminal Station's head house gleams in the summer sun. (Courtesy Warren Stephens, photographer.)

A row of Macon Transit Authority buses, coordinated to meet at Terminal Station to allow for easy transferring from one line to the other, prepare for their departures. Macon Transit Authority utilizes school-type transit vehicles for its less-busy routes, as seen here. (Courtesy Warren Stephens, photographer.)

A Gillig-built MTA bus reposes at Terminal Station on a beautiful August day in 2018. (Courtesy Warren Stephens, photographer.)

Terminal Station is utilized by the Macon Transit Authority for its downtown Central Transfer Station. The first buses leave the station at 5:45 a.m., and the last regularly scheduled bus leaves the station at 9:00 p.m. every weekday. (Courtesy Warren Stephens, photographer.)

Discover Thousands of Local History Books
Featuring Millions of Vintage Images

Arcadia Publishing, the leading local history publisher in the United States, is committed to making history accessible and meaningful through publishing books that celebrate and preserve the heritage of America's people and places.

Find more books like this at
www.arcadiapublishing.com

Search for your hometown history, your old stomping grounds, and even your favorite sports team.